The LIFE of the SOUL

The Path of Spirit in Your Lifetimes

As told through **JOHN McKIBBIN**
to **GATES McKIBBIN**

LIFELINES LIBRARY

For information, contact:

Field Flowers, Inc.
641 Healdsburg Avenue
Healdsburg, CA 95448
707 433 9771
www.fieldflowers.com
www.lifelineslibrary.com

Cover and text design by Kajun Design

Front cover detail from “The Three Stages of Life”
by Gustav Klimt (Scala/Art Resource)

Author’s photo by Christina Schmidhofer

ISBN 1-929799-04-7

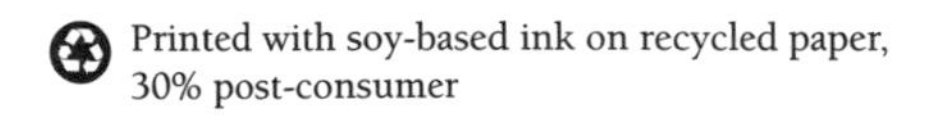
Printed with soy-based ink on recycled paper,
30% post-consumer

To my two soul sisters, Linda Davidson and Sally Hudson, who have been with me many times before—and are standing by me yet again—spiritually and otherwise

What began three years ago as a series of journal entries is now coming into the world as a series of books. All along the way people with the perspective and expertise I needed crossed my path at exactly the right time. Each person has contributed soul and substance to the project. I am abundantly grateful to:

- **Ned Engle**, who saw what my writings could become long before I did and then adroitly guided me there.
- **Barbra Dillenger, Michael Makay, Benjo Masilungan** and **Anthony Corso**, whose comments on each new manuscript reassured me of the accuracy and usefulness of the material.
- **Judith Appelbaum** and **Florence Janovic** at Sensible Solutions, whose savvy counsel about the publishing industry kept me confident and on course.
- **Carol Fall**, who offered discerning marketing advice and was the creative force behind the book titles.
- **Erin Blackwell** and **Cynthia Rubin**, whose editorial finesse honored and strengthened the messages.
- **Laurie Smith** and **Pat Koren** at Kajun Design, who transformed each book into a jewel within and without.

Also by Gates McKibbin:

The Light in the Living Room: Dad's Messages from the Other Side

LoveLines: Notes on Loving and Being Loved

A Course in Courage: Disarming the Darkness with Strength of Heart

A Handbook on Hope: Fusing Optimism and Action

Available Wisdom: Insights from Beyond the Third Dimension

CONTENTS

2 Glossary
5 Cosmology
10 Reincarnation
13 Karmic Relationships
17 Spiritual Evolution
19 Eternal Life
22 The Veil
24 Choice
27 Life Review
30 Love Patterns
33 Unconditional Love
35 Continuity
38 Time
41 Infinity
44 Gender
46 Oneness
48 Detachment
50 Surrender
52 Judging
54 Worthiness
56 Guidance
59 Remembering
61 Egolessness
63 Body, Mind and Spirit
66 Bridging
69 Cleansing
72 Patience
74 Character
77 Cosmic Forces
80 Coincidence
82 Inspiration
84 Flow
86 Nature
88 Wonder
90 Joy
92 Change
94 Benediction

GLOSSARY

Creation consists of multiple dimensions of reality. Each dimension is characterized by its vibratory or magnetic quality. The higher the frequency at which the dimension vibrates, the more at one it is with God. The **higher realms** are the dimensions of spiritual reality beyond the material world, where distinctions based on time and space do not exist.

Karma is composed of imprints on your soul created by your choices (thoughts, words and actions). Choices that embrace spirit heal, balance, complete and remove karmic imprints from your current and prior lifetimes that distance your soul from God. Choices that deny or avoid spirit add new imprints that must be healed, balanced, completed and removed later.

Your **lesson** is the larger karmic pattern or theme you are addressing during this lifetime.

Your **mission** is the major contribution you are making in this lifetime to enable the evolution of collective consciousness toward oneness with God.

Your **soul** is the vessel for your spirit. It carries an

infinite variety of karmic imprints that record the experiences your spirit has had, in and out of embodiment. Your soul is all love and light. It represents your limitless potential to embrace spirit to the fullest capacity.

Spirit guides are spiritual entities who have committed [illegible]ing you [illegible]ow the path of love and contribute to t[illegible] e[illegible]tion of all creation. They whisper in you[illegible]lly. They send you insights and intuitive [illegible]y reaffirm your deepest inner knowing that there [illegible] a benevolent higher power inherent in all things.

The **third dimension** is the material reality on planet earth. It consists of dense physical matter that vibrates slowly. The third dimension is characterized by segmented linear time (past, present and future) and compartmentalized space (measurements, boundaries and separation).

The **veil** is a magnetic field surrounding planet earth that separates the vibratory capacity of the third dimension from that of the higher realms. It forms a barrier between your earthly awareness and your higher consciousness. The veil creates the illusion that material reality—and your survival in it—is your reason for being.

The term **we** that is used throughout this book refers to John McKibbin, the spirit who was Gates' father in this lifetime, and the other spiritual entities collaborating with him on the messages he sent down to her.

COSMOLOGY

The cosmology on which this book is based describes the creation, evolution and maintenance of life in all of the universes. Its key assumptions are these:

- All of life stems from the Prime Creator*, whose spirit lives in everything that exists.
- That spirit has the potential of being the only influence affecting everything that exists. Living beings are currently fulfilling that potential to varying degrees.
- Creation consists of multiple dimensions of reality. Each dimension is characterized by its inherent oneness with God, reflected in its vibratory or magnetic quality. The higher-frequency dimensions are more at one with God.
- The spirit that is alive in all things never dies. It simply changes the form in which it is manifest as individual souls move in and out of physical embodiment.

---

* Prime Creator, God and the One are used synonymously.

- The soul is the vehicle for each spirit's progressions and transmutations through different forms. It carries memory imprints from the experiences that spirit has when it is embodied. It also carries the memory of its experiences between embodiments.
- The purpose of life is to create opportunities to make conscious choices that move the soul ever closer to God until oneness with the One is complete.
- All of life has infinite capacity to evolve toward the One.
- Planet earth, along with all other locations that life inhabits throughout the universes, exists as a theater providing opportunities for the evolution of souls individually and collectively toward enlightenment and oneness.
- The choices that people on earth face are rooted in the contradictions of duality. On the one hand, people must survive in the third-dimensional material reality of the body and the mind, with all of that dimension's inherent reasons to deny spirit. On the other hand, human beings are also vessels for spirit and thus have the capability to choose spiritual priorities over material ones. This enables their consciousness to move into the fourth or even higher dimensions while their souls continue to occupy third-dimensional bodies.
- Everyone in human embodiment is there because of his or her soul's decision to create a lifetime of opportunities to move toward spirit through conscious choice.
- Often people make unconscious choices that are

far from spirit-based. Their souls evolve slowly, if at all. Sometimes they make choices that cause their souls to move away from—not toward—spirit. Even then, spirit lives on within them.

- All of these choices produce residue on their soul, which carries these imprints from one lifetime to another. These soul impressions have been labeled karma.
- Most souls embodied on planet earth have experienced multiple lifetimes. Before taking embodiment, the soul energy plans the key choices it will have in the upcoming life experience. These choices contain the potential of moving toward light and love. Some are opportunities to heal or complete karmic patterns with another. Some are moral or ethical choices. Some provide the possibility of giving and receiving unconditional love and support.
- All thought and action produces imprints on the soul and impacts the physical and metaphysical reality that surrounds the individual. Each person has a hand in creating his or her own reality.
- Everything is interconnected because everything is at its essence God. All thought and action also influences the larger physical and metaphysical reality on this planet and others, in this solar system and others, in this universe and others. Thoughts and actions that move an individual closer to the One move all of life closer to the One.
- Thoughts and actions that are oblivious to or antagonistic toward spirit move the individual and all of life away from the One.

- This movement toward or away from God happens through magnetic vibration. All of life vibrates at a frequency commensurate with its own evolutionary state and that of all of consciousness.
- For millennia planet earth has been surrounded by a magnetic veil that has supported duality. The veil is required if people are to be free to choose. It keeps them from being either completely aware or completely unaware of the existence of the spiritual reality their souls left behind when they became embodied. This veil must be penetrable but not transparent. If it were impenetrable, individuals would be unaware of the existence of spirit and thus would have no choice to make. If the veil were transparent, the existence of spirit would be so obvious, people would incorporate it unthinkingly into everything they did. They, too, would have no choice to make. Evolution can occur only when beings face challenging decisions—ones where physical and metaphysical reality hang in the balance—and consciously select the most spirit-based option.
- The magnetic veil around the planet has remained fundamentally unchanged for many thousands of years, as souls individually and together made choice after choice, lifetime after lifetime.
- The potential outcome is that the veil would no longer be necessary because a sufficient quantity of people will have moved qualitatively close enough to spirit to create critical mass. Indeed, a critical mass of people has achieved this through their souls' own individual evolution, lifetime after life-

time. As a result, collective consciousness has shifted. The veil has been lifted.

This has almost unfathomable implications. More people will be able to access spirit more easily. Spirits in the higher realms will need to make fewer adjustments in their own magnetic field to work with you in the earth's dimension. You, in turn, will be able to rise above the limitations of your third-dimensional body consciousness to see, hear and feel us when we are with you.

You will be guided more effectively. You will be given more profound opportunities to recognize and make choices that honor the spirit that resides within yourselves and others. You will move rapidly toward spirit as you become more conscious with each thought you think and each action you take.

Our work with you has not ended, however. Quite the contrary, it has only begun. With the lifting of the veil, you face enormous responsibilities to integrate spirit more profoundly into your daily life. It is no longer an option to see life outside yourself as separate from yourself. It is no longer an option to create barriers between yourself and spirit in any of its manifestations.

But just as the responsibilities increase, so does the joy. As you grow closer to spirit, you will experience the deep inner peace that has eluded you for so long. You can integrate spirit more completely into your life.

The veil has been lifted. The magnetics surrounding the planet have shifted. The only thing holding you back is yourself.

Take the next step toward oneness. Then another. Then another.

The path is open to all.

REINCARNATION

Most souls in embodiment on planet earth at this moment have incarnated numerous times. This notion is in direct opposition to the theology of some religions, which hold that there is just one lifetime, after which the soul migrates to another place depending on how well you have comported yourself.

That is not what happens.

Why would God want to give you only one opportunity to "get it right?" Why would God establish rewards and punishments based on a seriously abbreviated chance for you to integrate the essence of spirit? Why would God stifle the evolution of your soul with just one lifetime? Why would God settle for anything less than your ultimate oneness with all of life, individually and collectively?

It is far more God-like to create a series of opportunities for you to evolve toward spirit. And that is exactly what God did.

Your soul is the vessel for your spirit in and out of embodiment. It carries an infinite variety of imprints from all of the experiences your spirit has had, in and out of embodiment. You realign the configuration of imprints on your soul with thoughts and actions. Choices that embrace spirit heal, balance, complete and remove karmic imprints that distance your soul from God. Choices that deny or avoid spirit add new imprints that must be healed, balanced, completed and removed later.

Your soul takes embodiment only after your spirit has committed to doing so. Underlying this commitment are your mission and lesson. Your *mission* is the major contribution you commit to making to enable the evolution of collective consciousness toward oneness with the One. Your *lesson* is the larger karmic pattern you will have the opportunity to address throughout this lifetime.

Your soul receives unlimited support for achieving its stated mission; its responsibility is to remain open to receiving that assistance, whatever form it takes. The opposite is true with regard to your lesson. The karmic imprints that define your lesson can be resolved only as a result of choices you make with no outside influence.

Souls in human bodies have made many previous choices that either ignored or negated spirit rather than honoring it. Their karmic imprints have multiplied, and thus the challenges their lessons introduce are formidable. Those imprints are a part of the soul's memory, but the magnetic veil around the planet has kept most people from accessing that memory.

Many of the people you encounter during your lifetime have shared other lifetimes with you. Key relationships almost invariably are grounded in one or more past lives. Some relationships present opportunities to address negative karmic patterns and resolve them. Others offer mutual support and reassurance. Your objective is to release the karma that you have accumulated during prior lifetimes without gathering additional imprints that you will have to release later.

See every moment in your life as an opportunity to cleanse and neutralize imprints and predispositions from past incarnations. The path to accomplishing that is the path of spirit—the path of unconditional love, service and sharing. It is the path of non-judging and non-attachment. It is the path of the living light.

You reach the end point when you have erased all karmic imprints from your soul. Then your soul is pristine and unencumbered. It is at one with the One. It embodies spirit, nothing but spirit.

At that point no more lifetimes are necessary. Your soul's journey continues, but along different directions and dimensions.

KARMIC RELATIONSHIPS

If your soul took embodiment for only one lifetime, it would not be necessary to carry forth the imprints from that experience into the higher dimensions once your soul left your body upon death. But your soul remains vibrant during and between many lifetimes. It records and transmits the influences from your thoughts and feelings, words and deeds. What it records is called karma.

All of the primary relationships that occur in each lifetime are karmic. You already know the key people you meet, even if you do not recognize them from before. You have shared prior experiences that are significant enough to have left a karmic imprint on your soul and most likely theirs as well. You have both arranged to meet each other again in this lifetime.

The objective of coming together once again will vary. You might have one friend with whom you share unconditional love effortlessly. In this instance, you both have agreed that your paths will cross so that you can offer mutual support and encouragement. You might have another friend with whom your relationship has been problematic. This enables you both to address the limitations, fears and judgments that you accumulated as a result of your relationship in a past life. As you neutralize these negative influences, you become free of karmic bondage. The same dynamics occur with your parents, siblings, children, relatives, colleagues, neighbors and others.

Karmic relationships fall into two categories:

- *Those that are rooted in love and light.* These give you an opportunity to strengthen your more enlightened karmic imprints and assist you on your journey toward spirit.
- *Those that are rooted in the opposite of love and light.* These give you an opportunity to reverse your unenlightened karmic imprints and also assist you on your journey toward spirit.

Both categories of karmic relationships are catalysts for the evolution of your consciousness. They both assist you on your journey toward spirit; they simply employ different means of doing so. Consequently, neither type of relationship is "good" or "bad," "positive" or "negative." They are equally effective in performing a critical function.

Relationships that require karmic healing and completion do not take you from your path. Quite the contrary. They provide you with built-in venues for doing your spiritual work. When you have forgiven the apparently unforgivable and shown deep compassion toward the apparently incorrigible, you feel more at peace. You know that within you are great reserves of love and light, and all you need to do is tap into them.

Your soul took embodiment to provide myriad

opportunities for you to deal with karmic unfinished business from prior lifetimes. What created this unfinished business? Given the choice between aligning your actions with spirit and doing the opposite, you opted for the latter. Thoughts, feelings and actions that deny the existence of spirit take the form of anger, revenge, intimidation, fear, oppression, greed, blame, violence and conceit. These choices feed off judgments, creating a hierarchy based on separation. They reinforce the illusion that some people are right and others are wrong.

Every time you fell prey to making choices that were devoid of spirit, your soul recorded the residue of that action. If under a similar circumstance you choose to act on the basis of love, you can release that residue. Doing so involves forgiveness, compassion, non-judging, detachment, optimism, generosity and open-mindedness—all of which must be unconditional.

Forgiveness, for instance, must be chosen with no other agenda than to forgive. Saying that you forgive someone in order to accomplish another purpose does not lead to forgiveness. It adds impressions to the soul rather than neutralizing the ones that were already there.

Keep in mind that karmic advancement is not automatic. There are no guarantees that your relationships will be any more spirit-based than the pattern you engaged in before. They may actually move you away from the light rather than toward it. You can either rise above the limitations or build upon the strengths you brought with you from prior lifetimes.

You can make progress only if you choose forgiveness over blame, faith over fear, optimism over anger, truth over falsehood, integrity over divisiveness, love over hate.

Expect to be tested to the limit by karmic relationships that need to be healed. They introduce powerful obstacles to your ability to embody love and light. They also introduce tremendous blessings into your life. For when you rise above your karmic predispositions, you take vast leaps forward on the path of spiritual evolution.

SPIRITUAL EVOLUTION

You evolve spiritually when your soul releases the earthly influences on your life and enhances the power of spirit. Devolution occurs when the opposite happens.

Your soul serves as a vessel for the results of your evolution or devolution—not as an active catalyst in bringing them about. Your soul cannot decide that since you are not evolving rapidly enough, it will nudge the process along by erasing karma that is holding you back. You alone, acting from your higher consciousness, can do that.

When your soul is in embodiment, it links spirit and practice. When it is out of embodiment, it does the same thing. What varies is the magnetic environment in which your soul finds itself. When your soul occupies your body on the physical plane, its magnetic frequency vibrates at a slower rate. When it leaves your body and enters the higher realms of spirit, it vibrates at a significantly higher frequency.

So although your soul links spirit and practice in the material and the etheric worlds, it functions differently in each. On the earthly plane your soul's purpose is to remind you of your karmic ties with former embodiments. It bridges practice (earthly choices that release you from karmic bondage) and spirit (faith in a reality beyond the earthly).

When your soul departs from your body upon death and enters the inner planes, it leaves earthly reality behind. The link between spirit and practice tightens. You are in service to spirit.

Your ability to be of service on the inner planes is enhanced by the progress you make on the earthly plane. If you spend your life accumulating karma rather than shedding it, your soul is overburdened with karmic residue when it leaves your body. The heavier the load, the more it hinders your spiritual effectiveness in the higher realms. Just as your physical body moves faster and more freely when you are lighter, so is your soul better able to transcend to dimensions farther and farther out when its karmic weight is reduced.

The more you are at one with spirit on the inner planes, the more capable you are of bringing that oneness with you when your soul takes embodiment again. This assists you in making spirit-based choices throughout your new incarnation. Those choices release karma and liberate your soul, enabling it to reach new heights when it leaves your body once again.

That is the cycle of spiritual evolution. The opposite process stimulates evolution in reverse. Whether you evolve or devolve is a function of how well you link spirit and practice, in and out of embodiment.

ETERNAL LIFE

Reincarnation presupposes that your soul lives on between lifetimes. And it does. That is what we mean by eternal life.

Your soul is your bridge through and between lifetimes. It is the vessel for spirit during every incarnation and after spirit leaves your body and moves to the inner planes. It is also the storehouse for karmic impressions that result from your experiences in and out of embodiment.

When conception occurs, your soul begins its progressive adaptation to human embodiment. During the gestation period your soul moves in and out of your physical body. There is no need for it to occupy your body permanently at that point, since it is not yet independent of your mother. Your mother's body provides the grounding for your soul, enabling it to move freely between the third dimension it will be entering and the higher dimensions it is leaving.

This is a time of preparation for the lifetime that lies ahead. Your soul has a great deal of work to do. This is the final opportunity to fine-tune the arrangements that need to be made for you to be given ample opportunity to address your mission and lesson. Your soul must use these last months wisely. After your birth your soul's ability to move freely between the third dimension and higher ones is greatly restricted.

Birth is a traumatic event not just because you must now function on your own physically, but also because your soul has less freedom to alternate between dimensions. A portion of your soul's energy enters your body permanently at birth. The rest of it flies free, enabling you to access the higher dimensions while you are in embodiment.

Thus your soul is the bridge between the lower and higher dimensions, even though a significant component of it has been committed to existence in your body.

During your new lifetime your soul provides the continuity between your current embodiment, past incarnations and the time spent in between lifetimes in the higher dimensions. Without your soul there would be no link between what you call past, present and future, in and out of embodiment.

So your soul's work is central to your evolution toward spirit. Your soul's manifestations throughout physical lifetimes and experiences in between them are the essence of eternal life. And the purpose of eternal life is the evolution of soul toward oneness with God.

During your physical lifetime you think and feel, speak and act. This creates impressions on your soul. Some impressions balance and thus neutralize existing ones. Some negate spirit and will need to be healed or completed later in the same lifetime or in other lifetimes.

Some embody spirit, raising the magnetic pattern at which your soul vibrates. All of these impressions act as soul memories.

When you experience physical death, your soul leaves your body, carrying your soul memories with it. Just as the soul spent nine months preparing for embodiment, it spends a similar length of time reviewing the life just completed. You conduct this review without judging. You refrain from labeling relationships or events, accomplishments or setbacks as being "right" or "wrong." The purpose of this review is to identify how far your soul moved in its evolution toward spirit and the lessons that remain to be addressed in lifetimes to come.

When this assessment is complete, your soul sets about its work in the higher dimensions. Your soul is not inactive when it leaves the body. Far from it. New challenges and assignments await. These experiences create impressions on your soul as well, adding to the memory bank that your soul brings with it into its next lifetime.

But that memory bank is not apparent or immediately available to you when you are in embodiment. The magnetic grid that separates the third dimension from all the others veils the memory bank from your conscious awareness. Your progress on the path to spirit raises the magnetic frequency at which your soul vibrates, enabling you to penetrate the veil more adeptly and thus tap into that memory bank.

Your soul is all love and light. It represents your infinite potential to embrace spirit to the fullest capacity. Your soul is the visionary within you.

Follow its lead. For in doing so, you will savor the delicious fruits of eternal life.

THE VEIL

What we call the veil is a magnetic field surrounding planet earth. This magnetism separates the vibratory level of the third dimension from that of the higher dimensions. It keeps you in material consciousness. It gives you the illusion that reality is composed of material things you can see and feel, and that your physical survival in that reality is paramount.

The veil separates your earthly awareness from your higher consciousness. Your material nature assures that your physical life is secure and your mental life is active. You must have food and shelter, learning and labor, family and community if you are to thrive in the world.

But you must also thrive spiritually. To invest all of your time and energy securing your physical existence is to turn your back on the reason you took embodiment. To have succeeded materially but not spiritually is to have not succeeded at all.

The two are not mutually exclusive. Being "spiritual" does not require you to live in poverty without subsistence. Nor does acquiring material wealth indicate that you are not "spiritual." If you sacrifice one for the other —if your body, mind or spirit becomes weak in the pursuit of your goals—you cannot achieve your full potential along any dimension. The means to spiritual evolution is to maintain a strong body, mind and spirit.

So the veil was placed around the planet to create circumstances that would give each soul in embodiment the opportunity to embrace spirit, love and light despite the strong pull of the material world. This requires faith in the existence of God and a willingness to set aside self-centered choices for those that benefit the many. Such choices fuel your soul's evolution and help you transcend the third dimension.

When the quantity and quality of your individual and collective choices reach critical mass, the magnetics surrounding the planet shift. The veil is lifted. The separation between material and spiritual reality becomes less extreme. Access to higher dimensions increases for all, and so does access to spirit.

CHOICE

Your soul's purpose in taking embodiment is to challenge you to make love-based choices that honor spirit despite the tide of opposite influences. To choose the immaterial in a world that worships the material—to remain attuned to the metaphysical in a world focused on the physical—is to take great strides on the path toward the One.

Your spiritual path is your means for achieving oneness with God. Steps on the path consist of choices—thoughts and feelings, words and deeds—that can move you closer to God. The choices you make every moment of the day have the potential of either making you more at one with God or distancing you from your Source. Those choices influence your spiritual evolution both incrementally and synergistically.

Each choice represents a separate, independent decision that you make at a particular moment in time. Making one choice under certain circumstances does not preclude your making the opposite choice under identical circumstances at another time. Over time, those choices have an incremental effect on your progress toward enlightenment.

More is involved than that, since the choices you make are also synergistic. They combine to create entirely new patterns and possibilities in your life. A quantum leap in your spiritual capacity can occur spontaneously when your choices—one after another, day after day, year after year—take you to a new threshold of oneness with God.

Every choice that you make also affects the vibratory magnetics of your physical and etheric bodies. Choices that dishonor spirit lower the vibration of your physical and etheric bodies, decreasing the frequency. They move you further away from spirit and embed you more deeply in the material world. They create broad chasms of separation between you and the rest of creation. They cover your inherent soul light with a thick layer of doubt and fear.

Love-based choices raise the frequency of the magnetic energy surrounding your body. They enable you to integrate the frequency of light into your body and let you sense your connectedness with all things. They make it possible for spirit to come closer to you and guide you more effectively. This guidance leads you to make even more spirit-based choices, which raise the vibratory level of your body and consciousness even more. In this way you move closer and closer to the One.

But the influence of your choices does not stop there. Those same choices also affect the collective consciousness of all humankind and, in fact, of all life. Since the spirit that lives within everything connects everything, your choices affect everything. The impact of every one of your thoughts, feelings, words and deeds is infinite. They alter the vibratory magnetics surrounding the planet and shift the overall vibration of all of creation.

No choice, no matter how small, is insignificant.

LIFE REVIEW

Your soul has taken embodiment many times. On each occasion, you planned in advance detailed opportunities for addressing karmic patterns and releasing barriers to your spiritual growth during that lifetime. You set aggressive goals for each embodiment in order to balance and complete your karmic pattern.

Each time your earthbound body dies, your soul leaves it behind and travels toward the light. That light is "home" to your soul. Its first task upon returning home is to engage in a straightforward, non-judgmental review of the lifetime you just completed. This is necessary in order to identify instances where you made karmic progress and where you either remained at the same place or regressed. Your integrity and humility during this review process are critical to an enlightened outcome.

This life review process is not focused on justifying your behavior after-the-fact. You are not in a courtroom with a judge and a jury. You have nothing to argue, nothing to defend. You are alone with your feelings, supported by your spirit guides and teachers. You look back on your life from an enlightened perspective. You see the bigger picture, understand connections that were not apparent to you before and recognize people you knew in earlier lifetimes who you thought were strangers this time around. You comprehend why you acted as you did and felt the way you felt.

You perceive events you took no notice of that were really breakthroughs—and situations that felt like breakthroughs but were actually setbacks. You know when your so-called unconditional love was conditional and when your caring for another was unconditional. You experience the extraordinary power of spirit that blessed you during the lowest points in your life and realize how what you believed to be the high points were often devoid of spirit. You marvel at the times you did your best and kept the faith despite the odds.

As a result of this assessment, you identify and celebrate the spiritual progress you made. You also pinpoint karmic habits that you were unable to break and areas where you consistently missed opportunities to grow spiritually. These are likely to be the focal points of your next life experience. You make note of them. Then you move on.

You do not dwell on the results of this life review. Its purpose is not to launch you on a guilt trip. Quite the contrary. Even if you made less progress than you had hoped when you began that lifetime, you are at peace. Out of embodiment, you can serve the God-force in many new ways. And you know that if you take embodiment again, you will have additional opportunities to address the remaining karmic challenges.

You do not have to wait until you leave the physical world, however, to review your current lifetime. You always have the option of taking a clear-headed look at the choices you are making and the impact they are having on your spiritual progress. The process can benefit you enormously.

LOVE PATTERNS

When you conduct your lifetime review after you have completed this embodiment, you will be looking at the love patterns in which you were engaged.

The expression of love in your life typically forms a pattern. Sometimes you alter the pattern from one relationship to the next. Sometimes it remains consistent across relationships. Whether the pattern is generic or idiosyncratic, it is indicative of how far you have come on the spiritual path.

There are four predictable love patterns:

- *Destruction,* total absence of love either for yourself or another
- *Competition,* love of yourself in the absence of love for another
- *Community,* love of yourself and others under cooperative conditions
- *Unconditional love,* love of yourself and others under all conditions

When you love neither yourself nor another, you destroy all potential for spirit to exist. You are guided by darkness rather than light. You see no possibility for growth or improvement, and you are weak with anger and hatred. You feel you have no latitude to alter the circumstances of your life or make it better for others. You are without hope. The future looks bleak. You are devoid of love. That is what makes the pattern destructive.

When you love yourself so much that you put your own benefit and gain above all else, you are being competitive. Your intention is to win as much and as often as possible while others lose, as much and as frequently as is necessary. You assume that everything that is desirable (including love) is available in a limited quantity, and that many people are out to acquire a large share of it. The goal is to accumulate the most while giving away the least. You win if you end up with more or all of the object of desire; you lose if you end up with less of it—or none at all.

Under cooperative conditions, love follows a pattern based on your willingness to forego individual gain either for mutual benefit with another or the greater good of the community. This must be agreed upon implicitly or explicitly. Behavior follows the pattern of conditional love: I give something if you offer something else in exchange. Everyone involved benefits. If the exchange is unfair or exploitative or one-sided, such mutual benefit is impossible. If in good faith you forego an individual benefit, only to have another person take it as his or her own, that is competition—not community.

Unconditional love has no agenda and serves no end result. It needs no reciprocity. It is complete unto itself. Unconditional love occurs naturally and spontaneously when spirit pervades a situation or relationship. It has no limits and undergoes no negotiation. It exits for no other reason than to be just what it is. Unconditional love is enlightenment in the material world, the spark of spirit with no source but its own.

Unconditional love can exist under any conditions. Whether you are in an environment of destructiveness, competition or communal cooperation, you can still choose the path of unconditional love. You are never required to compromise your ability to love based on the attitudes and actions of those around you. Finding it within yourself to love your destroyers or your competitors unconditionally is an opportunity for spiritual growth disguised as a challenge.

Take an honest look at the love patterns in which you are currently engaged. Which of the four patterns is most prevalent in your life? Why? Can you commit to unconditional love in one additional area of your life? If so, start immediately. If not, why not? Have you allowed yourself to fall to the level of the lowest common denominator that surrounds you, or have you been able to rise above it?

Be cognizant of the love patterns that determine your choices and influence your attitudes throughout the day. Remove the destructive ones. Transform the competitive ones into cooperative endeavors. Make more of the conditional ones unconditional. You will find that as you do this, you have far more love for yourself—and others—than you ever thought possible.

UNCONDITIONAL LOVE

Eternal life is eternal love. For without love, what purpose would eternal life serve?

As your soul evolves it is able to imbibe and embody love to a greater and greater degree. When your soul has reached its final destination, it is all love.

That is oneness with the One.

Love is available to you at all times. But what is called love in the third dimension may actually be more like a business arrangement: I will love you if you do something in return. That something in return might be to love me back. Sometimes it is more material than that: provide me with financial security, feed my ego, help me feel better about myself, protect me, maintain a measure of happiness for me. It is doubtful that much love, conditional or otherwise, is involved under these circumstances.

Unconditional love makes no such demands for reciprocity. To love unconditionally is to embody the essence of God. What is the essence of God? It is the acceptance of another without judging. It is the gift of enlightenment for the sake of sharing and expanding the light. It is faith that benevolence toward all is its own reward. It is trust that when one lives love, the rest will take care of itself.

Unconditional love is accompanied by overwhelming joy and quiet peace. It ushers in a sense of well-being and inner knowing that whatever is, is perfect. It is accompanied by surrender to God's will and commitment to serve God's purpose. It brings the profound understanding that you are God, and all other definitions of who you are matter little.

When you come from that place of knowing—that ability to embody unconditional love—you transform who you are in your third-dimensional reality. You see the light in others more easily and thus enable them to acknowledge it as well. You are kinder, more patient, more flexible, less ready to overpower others with your principles and perspectives. Your objective is to move closer and closer to light and love. If in doing so you set an example for others, so be it. But setting an example is not the purpose.

You love yourself. You love all. You are love.

CONTINUITY

To continue is to go on and on without stopping until completion has been reached. To continue is to maintain movement and momentum despite obstacles and setbacks. To continue is to take one step after another, even if the direction shifts.

Continuity requires you to be able to continue, but it is far more than that. Continuity is possible only if disparate components or diverse groups of people share something in common. If there is no common ground, there is no basis for continuity.

The source of the ultimate continuity—the common ground shared by all—is the God-force. This energy is alive in all things and cannot be extinguished. There is continuity of spirit throughout all of God's universes.

But how can such continuity affect anything if the presence of spirit is not apparent to all? How can there be spirit-based continuity if you are not even aware that spirit exists?

The continuity of the God-force does not require conscious awareness. It is present no matter what, just as spirit lives in everything no matter what. It makes possible the continuity of the soul.

Your spirit and soul are continuous; your life in physical embodiment is discontinuous. It has a beginning, middle and end. Living in the third dimension encourages people to segment their existence into slices of time and compartments of space. This segmentation is based on discontinuity—not continuity.

Spirit has no such linear reference point. It just is, always and everywhere. That beingness represents the highest level of continuity that is possible.

Your soul links the discontinuity of being in embodiment with the continuity of spirit. It carries the imprints of karma (based on discontinuous experience) and transmits the messages of spirit (based on continuity).

Without your soul, continuity from one lifetime to another would not be possible. Without that continuity the evolution of your soul would not be possible. And without the evolution of your soul, there would be no purpose to your life.

So you see, continuity is an essential component of God's plan.

This has implications for how you perceive day-to-day existence. If you believe that such continuity exists, then you will see the world holistically. Everything contains the seed of everything else. One event is connected to all other events. Whatever happens occurs because it is part of a larger evolutionary process.

God perceives all in a way that transcends your segmented approach to time and space. You too can do that when you set aside assumptions and mental structures rooted in material reality.

The principle of continuity is fundamental to all of God's work. Honor it whenever and wherever you can, for in doing so you are also honoring its source.

TIME

We have been giving you a great deal of information about the larger cosmic structure of things. However, this is to no avail if you attempt to understand what we are saying from a third-dimensional perspective of time.

Time on the physical plane is linear. It can be segmented into compartments that appear to represent what you call past, present and future. Your past is comprised of moments that have already occurred on that linear progression. They had a beginning, middle and end, all of which have concluded. You can retrace what happened, remembering it in great detail. You believe that whatever existed in your past cannot be altered or lived again.

Your present on the physical plane is occurring now. People have varying perspectives on the present. Some think of it as a minute, an hour or even a day. To others the present is a heartbeat, a blink of an eye, a moment too short to be measured. Most people refer to the present, but they are rarely conscious of it while it is flowing by them. Days and weeks go by without their being aware that they are creating their own reality moment to moment. They are so absorbed in recalling the past and anticipating the future, they miss the present altogether.

From a third-dimensional perspective, the future is all of time that has not occurred yet. The closer the proximity of those segments of time to the present, the more they impinge on your thinking. A man planning to retire in fifteen years will not go into detail yet about how he will spend his days. A woman anticipating a meeting in fifteen minutes is likely to spend that time reviewing the background information for it. As the future moves closer to the present, one becomes more acutely aware of the need to prepare for it, since soon it will become the past (and at that point nothing can be done to change it).

Or so you believe.

These segments you call past, present and future are reflective of third-dimensional material reality. Your past begins at the moment of your birth. Your future ends at the moment of your death.

Or so you believe.

But what if you acknowledge that the life of the soul is infinite; that your soul has already lived multiple lifetimes; that you carry within you the flame of spirit that existed before creation and will exist beyond forever? How would that influence the way you think about time?

At a minimum, you would need to expand the frame within which you place past, present and future. Your past would include all of your soul's experiences from the moment it emerged as God's creation. Your future would include all of your soul's experiences into infinity. Only the present would remain relatively the same, encompassing the time it takes to think a thought, feel a feeling, say a word or move a muscle.

So the continuum of time stretches in all directions from an infinitesimally brief moment, which constitutes the present as it is measured by liner time.

When you move beyond the third dimension, how is the past different from the future? In the higher realms what has already occurred and what is yet to occur become indistinguishable. They look the same, feel the same and carry the same magnetic energy. In the higher dimensions linear time does not exist. All that is, is one unified whole, all at once.

To repeat: All that is, is one unified whole, all at once.

Therefore, there is no time. Furthermore, there is neither "here" nor "there," so there is no space.

God's reality knows no time or space. Your soul's reality knows no time or space.

Remember that, the next time you are caught in a traffic jam or have a calendar laden with too much to do and too little time to accomplish it. Yes, you are living in the "real world," with all the demands it makes on your time and space. But you are also living in your soul's world, which makes no demands on your time and space.

Access that world in prayer and meditation, contemplation and gratefulness. Go there as often as you can.

It is home. It is God. It is you.

INFINITY

The literal meaning of the word *infinity* is not finite. If something is not finite, it has no beginning, middle or end, no starting or stopping point. The only parameter is that there are no parameters.

How could there be no parameters? We answer that question with a question: Why are they necessary?

Your third-dimensional way of seeing and being in the world requires you to divide time and space into manageable chunks. You segment time into nanoseconds, seconds, minutes, hours, days, weeks, months, years, decades, centuries, millennia. You compartmentalize space into squares and cubes, circles and spheres, triangles and cones. You then measure them in terms of linear or cubic inches, feet, yards, meters, miles and kilometers.

Such measuring and apportioning are necessary to preserve order in a material world. They are neither wrong nor superfluous. But they do come at a cost—the tendency to assume that everything else in creation is divided up in similar ways.

That is an inappropriate assumption.

All of God's creation is infinite. It all exists as one, all at once. The smallest atom contains the seed memory of an entire universe. The information from all of life is embedded in every cell. Everything that God is, is present in all things.

That is infinity.

Infinity is unfathomable from a purely material perspective. How can a universe be present in an atom? That is physically impossible, it would seem. How can a cell possibly store all the information that ever was? That is impossible, it would seem.

But when you release the need to think in terms of limited time and space and open yourself to the possibility that they may actually be limitless, then you might see that the largest intelligence can be retained in the smallest crystal. The most profound wisdom can be held in a snowflake. The movement of a galaxy can be embedded in a heartbeat. All of the love of God can be inhaled in a breath.

Do not try to understand infinity with your left brain. Its bias of rationality will resist accompanying you on your exploration. It will remind you of all the reasons infinity is preposterous, then it will make every effort to obstruct your discovery process.

Instead, open your right brain and your heart to infinity. Embrace all of God's universes with every movement of your body. Feel the pulse of all of life every time you close your eyes. Imbibe the light with every thought. Be grateful for the cosmic dance with every prayer.

Tap into infinity. Explore far beyond the boundaries of your day-to-day existence. See yourself as everything that God is; see your life as everything that God has created; see your purpose as advancing spirit in all of its manifestations.

You are not just you in your physical body at this moment in the history of planet earth. You are all of life throughout all of God's universes for all time.

You are, in a word, infinite.

GENDER

One of the requirements for taking human embodiment is that the soul must choose which gender the physical body will adopt for the lifetime to come. On planet earth gender is divided into male and female. The gender your soul chooses for each incarnation influences how you live out your karma and act on your mission. It is not an insignificant choice for the soul to make.

When you review the past lives from which you have brought the deepest karmic imprints into this one, you discover that in some of them you were a male and in some you were a female. Your experience of having been both male and female gives you a deeper understanding of the gender-based differences that have separated men and women over time. It also helps you understand how the other gender perceives the world, for you were that as well—many times.

This leads to a question many people ask: Is God male or female? The answer is, God is neither. God has no gender. God is both father and mother—the prime creative energy of all things. If God were one gender to the exclusion of the other, there would be something that God is not. And that is impossible.

The purpose of gender is to establish a baseline of difference that you are challenged to transcend. Beyond that, the diversity of the human race is considerable, although those differences are irrelevant in the realm of spirit.

When you understand this—and begin to live it—you have taken a huge step toward the One. You no longer judge others based on gender or race, height or weight, physical appearance or sexual preference. You see and feel the exquisite unity in diversity.

ONENESS

We refer often to oneness with God. The words sound nice, even inspiring. But what do they mean?

Oneness is the opposite of separateness. To be at one with another is to have erased all boundaries between yourself and the other to the point that there is no "other."

That is hard to imagine, for your reality is one of separateness. No matter how much in tune you are with another, no matter how much you lose yourself in union with another, no matter how much you try to be selfless, you still have a sense of being apart.

God knows no such separateness. Spirit is in everything and is everything. The One is one with all of creation. But reciprocally, all of creation is not at one with the One.

What hinders oneness? The belief that you are your material body surviving in a material world. The tendency to do whatever it takes to secure what you perceive to be your due. The inability to recognize that a life well-lived is one where the individual lives and breathes spirit.

Oneness requires you to surrender your life to doing

God's work. You will probably not be able to do that very well at first. You may not be able to do it at all at first. Start by asking yourself the following questions when you are about to make a decision or take action:

- What is the love-based way for me to approach the situation I am in at the moment?
- What is keeping me from acting in that way?
- What is the source of that limitation, and how can I transcend it?
- If I did just one small thing out of pure love right now, what would it be?

Then do it—and refrain from judging your effectiveness by the results you see.

Discard all sources of feedback about how well you are doing but one: your own sense of inner peace. All other input is irrelevant, for how can anyone else evaluate the quality of your own choice-making processes? How can another assess the degree to which you are integrating spirit into your life? How can anyone else experience the peace and joy that you derive from acting from spirit with no ulterior purpose?

Once you realize that the path to oneness with the One is solitary, you will find it easier to take step after step along the way. We are not saying that you must be alone in the world to be on this path. Quite the opposite. You must be an active member of your family, community and society. Within that context, you and you alone are responsible for the choices that will move you closer to the One. You make those choices by yourself, one at a time, day in and day out.

The light is bright. The path is open. It leads to oneness with the One. The journey starts with the first step.

DETACHMENT

Detachment is not about not showing up for your life, as many people think. It does not require you to take a passive role, to sit back and let things happen to you. Detachment is not synonymous with powerlessness or disillusionment.

Rather, detachment begins with your being fully present every moment of every day. You must be assertive and clear-headed about your purpose and goals. You must act from a place of love and light, over and over again. You must do everything in your power to be a messenger of spirit.

And then you must surrender the outcome of those thoughts, words and deeds to God.

If you cannot turn the result of your efforts over to God, you cannot achieve detachment. Trying to be detached when you actually prefer one outcome over another keeps you attached. Similarly, telling yourself that you should remain detached when you are lobbying to influence the outcome is counterproductive.

Detachment arises from non-judging. It is not a function of intellect; it is a matter of faith.

True detachment is rooted in three verbs: surrender, trust and accept.

To detach you must first *surrender* the results of your thoughts, words and deeds to God's will. That surrender assumes that whatever results from your best efforts is the most appropriate outcome, even if from your vantage point it appears to be a disaster.

You must *trust* that God's wisdom guides everything that occurs throughout creation and therefore can best determine what constitutes an appropriate outcome.

You must *accept* whatever occurs as deriving from the will of God. Do not question it. Do not rail against an unresponsive God who does not answer your requests or fulfill your most fervent prayers. Be grateful, no matter what the circumstances.

Show up, try your best and spread your light around. Ask for what you need and give every day all you've got. But do it with one thought in your head and one song in your heart: Thy will be done.

Thy will be done.

That is the mantra, and the essence, of detachment.

SURRENDER

Your understanding of surrender is competitive and in extreme instances, warlike. Surrender, you believe, occurs after defeat. Surrender signals loss of power at the hands of forces greater than those at your disposal. Loss takes other forms as well—loss of land, finances, culture, autonomy—none of which would be given up willingly under any other circumstances. Surrender is accompanied by shame, anger and regret. It is a last-ditch effort to salvage the minimally salvageable, which is usually life itself.

Those perspectives on surrender are the antithesis of what we mean here.

The catalyst for surrender is faith in a higher power with infinite wisdom and benevolence. When you surrender willingly and joyfully, you have transcended your spiritual limitations—not defeated them.

What do you surrender? You surrender the outcome of your actions and the need to control your future. You surrender the desire for assurance that what you believe is best or right will actually occur.

All of that you surrender to God. Yes, all of it.

That may seem unnecessary and perhaps even absurd. Why try to achieve an intended outcome, only to surrender the final result to a power outside yourself? Does that make any sense? Indeed it does.

Remember the purpose of being in this lifetime: to make choices that further your progress on the path to enlightenment. The situations in which you find yourself are opportunities to act with spirit and love. The immediate outcomes are irrelevant because the ultimate outcome you are trying to achieve is oneness with God.

You surrender to the will of God because that surrender opens the passageway to spirit. When you are incapable of such surrender, you close off a direct line to spirit. You sacrifice spirit for success and winning in the physical world.

What is there to win? Who is there to conquer? Do you want the spoils of battle and the assurance of peace bought with dominance and control? Or do you want peace that is born of oneness with the One, which translates into oneness with everyone?

Surrender is one of the most challenging aspects of the path to spirit. It goes against the mindset that puts survival and achievement first. But when you experience the surrender we are suggesting, your spirit is liberated from the need to dominate and control. You are free to be at peace—not keep the peace.

JUDGING

Many of your decisions are based on limitation and judging. Essentially you believe that you have a finite supply of resources, be they time, energy or money. When it comes to sharing those resources, you establish a hierarchy. The more deserving people are at the top, and the less deserving ones are in the lower echelons. The people closer to the top will get more or all of whatever you have in limited supply, and the others will receive little or nothing.

You might want to ask yourself, what is the most valuable gift you can bestow on anyone? Love. What limits your supply of love? The inability to access spirit in your daily life. And what keeps you from accessing spirit? Judging, among other things. If you release the tendency to judge others, you will be more capable of offering them love, which can flow freely through you in infinite quantities.

There is no limit to the amount of love that is available to you or anyone else. You are the only one getting in the way of such grace. God has infinite capacity to love; God has infinite love to give. God's love is available to all, without reservation, precondition or judging. You do not have to earn that love; you do not have to pass a test to receive it.

Why then should others pass your test before you can acknowledge, respect or love them? Who are you to judge them if God does not? How could you establish standards that are better or more appropriate than God's nonexistent ones?

Judging separates you from others and from spirit. It limits the love you embody and weakens your connection to spirit. There is no compelling reason to judge anyone, ever.

Disengage from judging everyone—businessmen in suits, beggars in rags and even yourself. Thoughts carry magnetic vibrations. Releasing your judgments shifts the energy field around yourself and others. That opens the passageway for the love vibration to flow to and through you.

Love and non-judging go hand-in-hand. They rise and fall together. When you eliminate your thoughts rooted in judging, you create more space for love.

WORTHINESS

You spend much of your time on the spiritual path feeling unworthy of enlightenment. The closer you come to spirit, the more you recognize how far away from God you have been. And that makes you feel unworthy. You recall all the times you acted from fear or frustration, and that makes you feel unworthy. Even when you are blessed, you feel unworthy. You ask yourself, why is God blessing *me?*

Worth is based on judging, and judging distances you from spirit.

God does not judge. God does not deem one person more worthy than another. God does not parcel out love in varying amounts based on your spiritual track record. God has no standards of excellence that make love unconditional for those who have "earned" it and conditional for those who have not.

Do not squander another moment feeling unworthy to receive God's love. For God loves all of creation equally. The last thing God wants is for you to establish a barrier to the limitless love that is available to you. And that is what you do when you believe that you are unworthy of it.

You may be acutely aware of your shortcomings as a child of God. You may know that for every step you take on the path you have followed a mile of detours off it.

Refrain from trapping yourself in a mire of self-judging. Instead, be conscious of your shortcomings when they occur, then shift the pattern. That is the process of spiritual evolution. It is also the path to God.

What could be more worthy than that?

GUIDANCE

Everyone in human embodiment has at least one spirit guide or teacher. This guide is a spiritual entity committed to assisting you on your path.

The parameters defining appropriate kinds of assistance are quite specific. On the one hand, support from your spirit guides must be relevant and enlightened. On the other hand, it must not release you from your karmic responsibilities or enable you to sidestep your karmic process. Your guides make judgment calls throughout the day regarding when to intervene and when not to, what to reveal to you and what to keep to themselves.

Most of the time you are oblivious to this guidance. You cannot see the entities that surround you, nor can you sense their presence. When a thought comes into your head, you believe that it is your own self-generated idea. You cannot imagine that the thought might have been sent to you telepathically by a spirit who is always at your side.

Spirits offer you guidance based on the mission and lesson you are pursuing in this lifetime. As we explained earlier, your *mission* states how you will contribute to the elevation of the collective consciousness and benefit of the greater good. Your *lesson* is the karmic theme you are addressing—the most effective path you can take to balance, heal and complete thoughts, feelings, words and deeds from previous incarnations.

Spirit guides can give you unlimited assistance as you work to achieve your mission. They have no latitude, however, to do or say anything that might interfere with your lesson. Their task is to be clear about the difference and to act accordingly.

But even their mission-based assistance is not automatic. They cannot support you in achieving your mission if you are not committed to it.

You might ask, how can I be committed to my mission if I don't know what it is? Ask your guides for help, then sit quietly and listen. Ask yourself, then sit quietly and listen. The words will come to you. Do not wonder if the words are from a spiritual entity accompanying you or from your own soul. There is no difference, really.

After you have articulated your mission, commit to it—every morning when you wake up, every night before you go to sleep, as often as you want, whenever you want. Commitment opens the pathways for spirit to shower you (and sometimes flood you) with guidance. The only thing getting in the way is your unwillingness to receive it.

You can also talk out loud to your guides about the challenges you face as you pursue your lesson. They have the latitude to offer telepathic insights but cannot provide you with information enabling you to sidestep the process of completing your karma.

Your lesson is not just to learn how to deal with your karmic predispositions, but to transform those tendencies into choices that embody spirit. When you do that, you release the less enlightened karmic imprints you brought with you from other lifetimes.

There is no shortcut to this end; there is no detour that allows you to avoid doing your karmic work. And your guides most certainly cannot do it for you.

Your guides are always with you. They collaborate with you when you are asleep and your higher consciousness is released from the bondage of your body-consciousness. They ride with you on the bus and in your car. They attend meetings with you, cook meals with you and throw parties with you.

Acknowledge their presence, even if you cannot sense them. Invite them into your ruminations and explorations. Ask them out loud for help. Express your gratitude for their presence in your life. You have exceptional support with what matters most.

REMEMBERING

Your guides help you remember what you already know. But how can it be called remembering if it often seems as if you are learning things for the first time? Have you forgotten significant principles and guideposts?

You have not forgotten anything. The knowledge has stayed with you; you just have not yet been able to access your memory of it.

When you turn your computer off, it does not lose the information you have saved on the hard drive. You can access it when the computer is re-energized with electricity.

Your spiritual memory is like that. You carried it with you into this embodiment. You merge with it every time your consciousness leaves your body, in the sleep state. You experience it when you go into a deep contemplation and feel utter peace and joy. You tap into it when you engage in guided meditations that enable you to relive past lives.

In all of these instances, you are plugging into the magnetic energy of the God-force, which enables you to access your spiritual database. Empower your spiritual memory to inform, inspire and guide you.

You already know everything you need to know, but you rarely do what it takes to remember it. Make the process of remembering a priority in your life.

EGOLESSNESS

Your ego's reason for being is to keep you successful and secure in the material world. Without it you would have difficulty functioning. It holds your third-dimensional self together as you maneuver through the vicissitudes of daily living. It wards off assaults from a variety of sources such as unrealistic expectations, competitive relationships and closed-minded judging.

Indeed, your ego plays a critical role in your life. But its services come at a considerable price: keeping you wedded to your physical reality. The more you involve your ego in getting through the day, the more it distances you from spirit. Because the biggest threat to your ego is your spirit, your ego moves as far away from it as possible.

Why is the ego so threatened? When you surrender to the will of God, when you devote your life to service, when you make decisions based on faith in the wisdom of the One, you find that you need your ego very little. And because the ego thrives on being needed, the more you imbibe spirit, the more resistance you can expect from your ego.

That resistance is often quite subtle. You may receive a message from one of your spirit guides that inspires you to take a leap of faith. Almost immediately your ego begins to whisper doubts about it: "That is a ridiculous idea! It would never work. There is no reason even to try it. Why waste your time? Be reasonable and avoid the risk. You have more to lose than to gain by doing that." Your ego persists until you forget that the inspiration ever occurred.

Let your ego build the self-confidence you need to hold your own in the world. But do not become so enamored of its definition of who you are that you discount the central role of spirit in your life.

You need to thrive and prosper both in the material world and the realm of spirit. To do the former, you must call on your ego often during the day. Acknowledge the many ways it serves you. Keep it balanced and healthy, but do not let it overpower everything else.

Understand that you are far more than a physical person living the material existence your ego supports. Slow down. Simplify. Listen to the silence. Create solitude. Give yourself the gift of inner stillness and peace. That is where egolessness dwells. It is also the home of spirit.

BODY, MIND and SPIRIT

All of God's universes are one, yet each is separate and distinct. Some have life that is predominantly rocks and minerals. Others have life that vibrates at such a high frequency, it is close to being at one with God.

Every life form contains within it all of the vibratory frequencies occurring in all of the universes. What varies is the dominant magnetic vibration. The terms *higher* and *lower* frequency do not imply that the former is better. For God values no one aspect of creation more than another.

God loves everything in all of the universes with equal depth and devotion. God's gift to all of life is unconditional love. God's love lives within all that is in the form of light. This light vibrates at varying frequencies, depending on your oneness with God. As your soul moves closer to oneness, the magnetic frequency at which your body, mind and spirit vibrate becomes faster and faster.

Typically your body vibrates at the lowest frequency because it is the densest in composition. Your mind is next. Your spirit vibrates at the highest frequency. Nonetheless, all three must be aligned at the lowest frequency —your weakest link to spirit.

This alignment is dynamic, however. When you meditate or pray, your spirit soars to such a place of love, your body and mind follow along. When your mind is under considerable stress and your body becomes ill, your spirit also becomes weak. Body, mind and spirit are in a constant state of flux, and that fluctuation is within your control.

Let's say, for instance, that your body could not be in better shape. You make choices that strengthen its systems and slow its deterioration with age. But your mind is weak from life circumstances that you resist addressing. They prey on you whenever you stop long enough to allow them into your thoughts. No matter how perfect a temple for spirit your body is, your mind is almost incapable of integrating spirit. Concomitantly, you can lead an active, positive mental life, but if your body is unattended, it seriously limits your overall vibratory capacity.

You choose what food, drink and other substances you put into your body. You choose how much you exercise, how many hours of sleep you get, how hard you work, how much rejuvenation time you build into your day. Even though your body vibrates at the lowest frequency, you have enormous latitude to keep it healthy and free of impurities. That builds your capability to be a physical vessel for spirit.

Your mind is influenced by the thoughts and feelings that you allow into it throughout the day. If you occupy your mind with worries and concerns, fears and frustrations, you fill it with low-frequency vibrations. They in turn make it impossible for spirit to vibrate at a higher level. If instead you maintain a mental attitude of love and compassion, joy and serenity, spirit is able to align itself with a significantly higher level of consciousness. You are as responsible for maintaining optimism and mental vitality as you are for keeping your body strong and healthy.

Your spirit must also be vital and loving. Contemplation and reflection, meditation and prayer are exercise for your spirit. So are actions rooted in generosity and compassion. When you reaffirm your serenity, whether it is through solitary stillness or love-based deeds, you nourish your spirit. Just as you feed your body and provide your mind with food for thought, you must also feed your spirit with opportunities to tap into the God-source. Keeping physically and mentally fit, only to avoid endeavors of higher consciousness, does little to carry you further on the path to spirit.

Your responsibility as a child of God is to nurture and strengthen your mind, body and spirit. In doing that you honor yourself and your Creator.

There is no more noble cause than that.

BRIDGING

Your mind has an almost infinite capacity to resonate with the material world—to be body-conscious. After all, it is located in your body and is integral to the functioning of your body. It understands the earthly reality in which your body must survive and stimulates your incentive to thrive physically.

But your mind can do far more than that.

At the other end of the continuum is your mind's ability to be at one with spirit. When you are one-pointed in prayer or contemplation, when you have cleared your mind of the clutter and chatter of the moment, your mind locks onto the wavelength of spirit. You feel at peace and experience serene joy. You also sense an exalted awareness of who you are and why you are here, even if you cannot define or label it. Sometimes that spirit-based consciousness manifests in your body as a rush of emotion, chills or tears.

Because of your mind's dual capability, it is uniquely able to bridge body and spirit. That is quite a wide chasm. Your mind can bring your spirit down to the earthly existence of your body or bring your body up to the more rarefied habitat of your spirit.

Your mind is able to bridge body and spirit because it can ground itself in both. A bridge that is not well fortified at both ends of the span cannot provide adequate assurance that the path between the two is secure. If the bridge's foundation on one side is strong, but has only a temporary structure on the other side, it is unsound. The ability of your mind to tap into your spirit and body equally is essential.

Think about the role of a bridge. It assures you at the point of departure on one side that there is a landing point on the other side. In between it offers you footing across a distance where there originally was none. It creates the assurance and confidence you need to transport yourself into what would otherwise be thin air. It implies that if you left your roadmap on one side, another one will be waiting for you when you get to the other side.

And not inconsequentially, a bridge provides a way back. You are not required to leave one reality behind permanently when you step onto the span. You may go back and forth across the span as often as you want.

Think of your mind as serving that function in your life. It keeps you in your body throughout the day. It also brings spirit into your consciousness throughout the day. Both are essential.

If you live a totally physical existence, devoid of spirit, you lose touch with your reason for being. If you spend your time so at one with spirit that you lose touch with your body, you become vulnerable to the innumerable ways you can be at physical risk.

Maintain your mind with infusions of spirit and

inspiration, intellectual stimulation and challenging perspectives. Give it oxygen from physical exercise and nutrition from healthy food. Love your mind and the critical role it plays in your life. Allow it room to innovate and explore. And remember to be grateful for the bridge it provides.

CLEANSING

To follow the path of spirit is to cleanse your soul of karmic residue gathered from your actions during your current and previous embodiments. That karmic cleanup is the purpose for your taking embodiment. The more of it you do, the more you are able to live in love and light, and thus move closer to God.

The process of clearing out karmic impressions is mirrored in your daily life. Direct parallels between the karmic baggage your soul is saddled with and the mundane baggage you saddle yourself with may seem absurd to you at first. After all, being spiritual and being a packrat are not mutually exclusive, are they? No, not in the absolute. But the amount of clutter you surround yourself with is an indicator of the degree to which you are probably being distracted from your path.

Clutter in your life takes many different forms. The most obvious clutter is material—too many things, whether they are books, clothing, tools or toys. But there is also verbal clutter—overly long conversations, obligatory meetings, mass media chatter. And there is mental clutter—worries about the future, regrets about the past, frustrations with the present. Finally, there is psychic clutter—unresolved conflicts, unforgiven betrayals and unforgotten resentments.

Clutter in any of these aspects creates barriers to your spiritual progress, draining you of energy for spirit and robbing you of time with spirit.

If you have a great many things, you probably had to earn money to acquire them, take time to select them, invest effort in maintaining them, arrange for a place to store them and finally, dispose of them when you no longer need them. Little of that activity is likely to be conducive to being with spirit. If you are busy earning money to buy things, then using them, repairing them, storing them and throwing them out, peaceful interludes with spirit are likely to be few and far between.

Let's say that you do remove this clutter from your life and when you sit quietly your mind is filled with fears, doubts and concerns. That mental clutter will provide just as effective an obstacle to spirit as the material things you cleared out of your life. The same is true for psychic clutter. In fact, in order of impact, psychic clutter is the weightiest, followed by mental, verbal and material, which is actually the least ponderous.

Systematically cleanse your life of all types of clutter. Start with the easy cleaning first.

The next time you are shopping and see an item that is nice but not essential, refrain from purchasing it. Do that again and again. Then use the money you have saved on something that feeds your soul. Or ask yourself if you really need to invest such effort earning so much money.

Simultaneously, start evaluating everything you have

around you and releasing what you do not really like, need or want. Get it out of your life.

Reduce the time you spend in superfluous conversation, subscribe to fewer magazines and reconsider whether you want to continue relationships that deplete you. Then use the moments you have freed up, whether they are minutes, hours or days, to sustain your soul. Use the energy you have released to do something that maintains love.

Mental and psychic clutter are far more difficult to contend with, for they are more insidious and tenacious. They require constant attention. You might set aside a worry, only to discover that it has not really gone away. It has only gone backstage.

There are no easy approaches for dealing with mental and psychic clutter, but it is possible to neutralize them over time. Start by recognizing when this clutter has appeared. Take a look at its source. What is keeping you from releasing your worry, fear or anger? What can you do to influence the situation or bring it to closure? If it is out of your hands, turn the process and outcome over to God. Each time you do that successfully, you unburden your mind and heart, which then creates room for spirit.

Lighten the load. There is no need to carry it around any more.

PATIENCE

Once you start on the spiritual path and taste its fruits, you are likely to grow impatient. You will want to make great strides, quickly. You may be tempted to drop out of the world so that you can spend every waking moment in touch with spirit. You may cancel your life plans and walk away from your responsibilities in order to follow a higher calling.

You may well be acting from devotion to a higher calling. Or you may be acting from impatience. It behooves you to know the difference.

The spiritual path requires extraordinary patience, for you are not likely to see immediate results from your dedication to spirit.

Initially your life might become more rather than less challenging. Proceeding on your path means addressing entrenched karmic patterns, and that is difficult work. You will be tested, then tested again. As you progress, the tests become greater—not easier.

All of this will try your patience. Why would you do this, if all it leads to are more challenges? Wasn't life a lot easier before you decided to embark on your spiritual journey? When will you have some proof that it is worth the trouble? Impatience entices you off the path.

The opposite dynamic can also occur. Let's say that you do begin to experience living more wholly in spirit. You have respites when you know to the depths of your soul that everything is as it should be, and it is perfection. You are more loving and compassionate and forgiving. You experience bliss. You think, this is great! I want more of it and I know just how to get it!

So you attack your spiritual life with a vengeance. You work at it constantly. You meditate daily, refrain from negative thoughts and pick yourself up when you get off-track. You become a spiritual over-achiever. When you sense that your transgressions are slowing you down, you blame yourself. You've got the formula; you know the drill. Why can't you stick with it? You long to be all spirit, but you are spirit in a human body. Your impatient desire to move toward spirit ends up keeping you further from it.

Impatience arises from misalignment between your actual progress and your perception of what it ought to be. That misalignment arises from judging and preconception. The results you achieve will not follow a predictable timeline or a linear trajectory. There will be periods of apparent standstill, followed by quantum leaps. Patience is critical right before the breakthroughs.

In addition, reconsider how you are evaluating the results you see. Increasingly difficult challenges as well as more sublime experiences can both be indicators of your exceptional spiritual progress. Accept whatever occurs as the next opportunity to evolve toward spirit. That will reaffirm patience instead of its opposite.

CHARACTER

Character has different meanings based on context. Saying that someone is a character implies that he is eccentric or has an unusual personality. A woman who has character distinguishes herself from others through her wisdom and thoughtful actions.

It takes character defined both ways to pursue the path of spirit. To embody light is to be guided by spiritual wisdom and thoughtfulness toward all of humanity. That requires you to make love-based choices, even (or perhaps especially) in circumstances that defy you to do so. That is the essence of character.

Further, when you embrace spirit as the central reality of your life—when you refrain from judging in a judgment-filled world—you will probably be perceived by others as a real character.

The spiritual path is not for the faint-of-heart. It puts you in the minority and requires a level of self-assurance that is not necessary for following a more conventional path. Nor does this self-assurance derive from ego, which creates the illusion of it in order to disguise a sense of vulnerability. Instead, it derives from unwavering commitment and profound inner knowing.

The self-assurance that serves you best is not dependent on what others think of you, or say about you or say to you. It comes from what you know—and say and think and feel—deep within yourself.

That is character.

Having character is a by-product of the quality of your presence in the world. You cannot set out consciously to have character, for in calculating that desired end, you make it unattainable. You cannot make yourself wise by trying to act with wisdom when you have none. You cannot be humble when your ego is telling you to impress people with your humility. You are not really on the spiritual path if you are doing so either because it is the latest craze—or isn't.

So when we say that it takes character to live a love-based, light-infused existence, we are reminding you that to do so requires wisdom and humility. And the only source for either is within.

Each step on the path occurs because of a choice you and you alone can make. It takes wisdom to recognize those steps; it requires courage to take those steps; it takes humility to be grateful for the opportunity to do so.

As you become more at one with spirit, you will recognize an inner transformation. You will be more at peace with who you are and how you are living your life. You will consume less, whether it is food, conversation or the daily news. You will simplify, pare down, clear out, throw away whatever is no longer necessary. Your environment will become more harmonious, as will your relationships.

You may appear to others to be quite a character. You will also embody what it means to have character. Both will suit you well.

COSMIC FORCES

You exist in the context of your own karmic imprints, which are the sum total of your choices during your previous lifetimes and the current one. You also live in the third-dimensional reality of planet earth, with its political, economic, social and environmental dynamics. And finally, you are interconnected with a larger cosmic reality, one that integrates all of life and spirit into a holistic unity.

All three of these influences impact your life. You come into contact with people whom you knew before in other lives in order to balance and heal your karmic relationships. You spend your days making the best possible choices you can. You also influence and are influenced by the unseen dynamics of the higher dimensions.

Those cosmic forces affect you far more than your own karmic history and the dynamics of the material world.

Try thinking of yourself in the context of cosmic forces in this way. You are a grain of sand on a beach composed of many other grains of sand. That beach is part of a natural molecular mass (the planet) that has many other beaches with many other grains of sand. Those grains of sand move about constantly with the tides, which are determined by the phases of the moon. The moon is linked with a planet in a larger solar system that revolves around a sun in a universe with many other solar systems in a totality composed of many other universes.

There you are, that single grain of sand with all of your karmic and material challenges, being tossed around on the beach during high tide and left to dry in the sun during low tide. The force of the tides is much more powerful than you are. The draw of the moon is much more powerful than the tides. And so on.

This gives you an idea of the extraordinary influence of the cosmic forces on everything that happens day-to-day during your life on planet earth.

Beware not to take the metaphor of the sand and the tides too literally, however, for doing so would make you feel buffeted about mercilessly with no ability to influence the course of your life. That is as far from the truth as anything could be.

The point we are making is this: You believe that the most effective way to improve your life materially and spiritually is to knuckle under and get the job done. That is not a bad idea, but it represents only about fifteen percent of what you could be doing. If you are spending most of your day engaged in such activity, you are missing the best opportunities that are available to you.

Instead, tap into the cosmic forces and ride those waves. How do you do that? First you have to learn how to "swim" by using the discipline of meditation, contemplation or reflection. Then you must learn to "read the ocean"—your intuition or inner knowing. It flows with the cosmic forces and is in tune with their messages. Finally, you must have the courage to ride the waves. Act on the guidance you receive from spirit. Do so with confidence and conviction.

Then you will no longer be simply a grain of sand on the beach. For infinite moments you will be at one with the ocean, the moon and the solar system, the universe and all other universes.

For infinite moments you will be at one with the One.

COINCIDENCE

The root meaning of the word *coincidence* is easy to decipher: co-incidence, two or more happenings occurring simultaneously. The term is used to refer to a situation involving an unlikely intersection of two events, with the emphasis on *unlikely.*

What appears to be unlikely from a third-dimensional viewpoint is completely predictable from the higher dimensions. We see the larger patterns that guide the flow of events. We focus on patterns, not the events themselves. You see individual events without recognizing the larger scheme in which they are embedded. So when two things happen together that could not have been planned or predicted, you take notice.

And you should. Coincidences are special messages that nudge you out of your current framework. They signal that something bigger is at work. They serve as a wake-up call when you are sleepwalking through an important moment in your life.

Another word for coincidence is synchronicity. *Synchronous* means in-synch timing. The source of this quality of being in-synch is beyond the third dimension. Something random occurs out of the blue (although it is neither random nor out of the blue) and you ask yourself, "What was that all about?"

What that was all about is the bigger picture. You may be limiting the scope of your involvement in something or falling back on former behavior patterns. You may be off-track in your assessment of a situation or fragmented in the way you are approaching an issue.

Suddenly something synchronous occurs, and all of the constructs you are using are called into question. You see the situation in a new way, with fresh eyes and sharper lenses. You know that there is a bigger picture, and even if you cannot see exactly what it is, you are more ready to discover and accommodate it.

The paradox of coincidence is this: On the one hand, coincidence is not random. It represents the intricate design of life and embodies the interconnectedness of all things. From the perspective of higher consciousness, coincidences are eminently predictable.

On the other hand, they cannot be planned, managed or willed into being. You cannot say, "There is something bigger going on here. To prove it, I am going to make a coincidence happen."

Instead, understand that when one occurs, you have been blessed with a message that you are on a track that warrants reconsideration from your highest level of knowing. Then take the time to revisit all aspects of it. The results may surprise you.

INSPIRATION

The literal meaning of the word *inspire* is to intake or imbibe spirit, to be stimulated by spirit. Inspiration is communion with spirit.

You cannot plan inspiration into your day: 9:00—Be inspired, 9:15—Create preliminary draft based on inspiration, 10:00—Present plan to implement inspiration.

You cannot will it into being by thinking, I will be inspired by the symphony performance I am attending tonight.

You cannot beg for inspiration or demand it or trick it into appearing.

Instead, inspiration arrives on the wings of spirit, gracing you with its presence.

Inspiration is a constant potentiality, for spirit surrounds you and is within you. When you are inspired, spirit has found a new passageway to you. It has brought you a fresh insight or has expanded your ability to love.

Inspiration is an affirmation that at the moment it arrives, you are at one with God. You transcend your material reality and open up to spirit to the extent that during that brief yet timeless inspiration, you are all spirit. You are in-spirit.

The magnetic vibration of inspiration is aligned with the higher planes. When you are inspired, you are bringing down information from those planes through the magnetics of spirit. That information is rooted in the larger patterns of the cosmos. Inspiration transmutes that knowledge into a thought or a breakthrough that can be received—and acted upon—on the physical plane.

The power of inspiration is not just that it comes from the spiritual reality of the inner planes. Rather, its power is in the translation of that state of being into one that is compatible with human life on earth. For inspiration without translation would be of no value. Inspiration that could be neither integrated nor enacted would have little impact.

Often inspiration arrives when you least expect it. Notice what you are doing when you receive a special message from spirit. You might be taking a shower, walking or gardening. Your mind is clear and relaxed. You are physically rested, and you are effortlessly in the flow of things. Then suddenly, there it is—a word, a new insight or a breakthrough. You just had a visit from spirit.

Honor those visits and the perspectives they provide, for their guidance is invariably on target. Recognize under what conditions inspiration occurs and when it eludes you. Cultivate the open mind and heart that enable you to receive spirit, to be inspired.

FLOW

We use the phrase *in the flow* to refer to being plugged into the movement and dynamics of the higher dimensions. When that occurs—when the rhythms and realities of your daily life lose their prominence—your efforts become effortless. You are focused on what you are doing. But rather than trying to make it happen, you allow it to flow to and through you. You become a vehicle for higher-dimensional influences to manifest in the third dimension.

Flow is a byproduct of inspiration. It is a gift from spirit—an opportunity to experience the more ethereal realms of consciousness while you remain in embodiment.

To arrive at the flow state, you must set aside the attitudes and predispositions that keep your body in the third dimension, such as:

- Preference for one result over another
- Concern about how others will judge you
- Anxiety over the implications of your actions
- Desire to prove something to someone
- Need to conceal your sense of inadequacy

The list goes on and on. It is not easy to leave such thoughts and feelings behind. They nag at you and nip at your heels. Yet if you cannot quiet these voices of doubt and limitation, they will fill the silence and keep you from the flow.

To learn how to get into the flow of things, start with something you love to do that you do well. It could be cooking, carpentry, sewing, writing or painting. Allow ample time to relax into the creative process. Avoid starting off with any preconceived notions of what you are creating. Give yourself permission to play around with ideas and forms, themes and patterns. Do not evaluate your progress along the way. Just allow yourself and your creation to be.

You might embark on a different direction without knowing—or even caring—where you end up. You may feel as if someone else is influencing the process. You witness yourself creating your best work, yet it is as if you were not doing it at all. At that moment you are in the flow. You have made the space for spirit to work through you.

Once you experience what it means to be in flow, you will be able to return there more easily and more often, even when you are working in areas where you have less expertise or capability. There are no limits to the amount of time you can spend there.

NATURE

Nature is effortlessly at one with spirit. Ecological cycles mirror the higher order to which all of life is inextricably linked. Natural phenomena are integrated at the planetary level and woven into the larger magnetic patterns of the universe. It is impossible to do one thing in nature that does not have ramifications somewhere else.

Nature has no karma to work through. It is not concerned about past, present or future. For those reasons, nature may seem to be disconnected from human life. It may appear that the laws of nature are irrelevant to the lives of people.

Nothing could be further from the truth.

Nature is at one with all of life in all of God's universes. People are at one with all of life in all of God's universes. And people are at one with nature. Every choice you make impacts nature, and every natural occurrence impacts your choices.

You might assert that people have consciousness and intelligence, which are lacking in nature. Did it ever occur to you that the consciousness and intelligence in nature may be far more spiritually evolved than anything human beings demonstrate?

After all, there is no separation between nature and God. Nature is God.

The environmental destruction that has occurred on the planet in the last two centuries is the result of human choice. The unprecedented natural upheavals that throw regions of the planet into disequilibrium reveal the larger impact of your choices.

Do not make the mistake of believing that natural occurrences have nothing to do with you. They have everything to do with you. If nature is out of balance, so are you. If you progress rapidly toward your own spiritual healing, nature heals as well.

Nature provides you with a beautiful environment that also functions in perfect harmony with the God-force. When you honor nature, you also honor yourself. When you honor and respect nature and yourself, you also honor God.

That is the natural order of things.

WONDER

Wonder springs forth when you come face-to-face with the existence of spirit manifest on the physical plane. Natural phenomena inspire wonder, whether it is an opportunity to recognize the perfection of a dewdrop on a rose or the magnificence of a mountain range. Architecture, superb art and intellectual discoveries can stimulate the same response.

To be capable of wonder requires you to stop what you are doing or thinking long enough to give attention completely to something else. You must open your senses and your aesthetic appreciation to what is before you. Wonder asks that you be fully present, without prejudice. Only then can you witness spirit in its entirety, as it resides in awe and wonder.

Wonder, then, derives from embracing what exists so completely that you become one with the spirit that is inherent within it. To observe something while remaining separate from it prevents you from accessing its spirit. It also keeps you from appreciating its essence fully—if at all.

You do not need to travel to the Himalayas or go to a museum to bring wonder into your life. The opportunity to be full of wonder is everywhere around you, all the time.

How do you tap into wonderment?

- ♦ Reduce the impact of stimuli in your environment, whether they are interpersonal, technological or mental.
- ♦ Slow down for brief periods every day.
- ♦ Stop long enough to observe something with complete attention and appreciation.
- ♦ See with your ears, hear with your eyes, touch fragrances, smell textures.
- ♦ Pinpoint your focus in order to attend to every detail of something, then relax into the essence of it, becoming what it is.
- ♦ Discover with the innocent wisdom of a child.

JOY

We have been focusing on the mechanics of spiritual evolution—the underlying structure and function of the cosmos.

But if you take a totally prescriptive or mechanical approach to the process we are describing, you have missed the point. God did not establish this complex set of circumstances in order for you to shoulder a ponderous burden. The purpose of spiritual evolution is to unburden you—not to keep you on a perpetual treadmill that goes nowhere.

Yes, you do face extraordinary responsibilities, and the only way to lay down your karmic baggage is to bring your karma to completion. Yes, you will be tested over and over again on your path to spirit. You will be confounded, you will doubt, you will grow weary of the journey. But even then, the process we are describing can be one of joy.

Joy is your built-in navigational system. It is available at all times to keep you on course as you traverse the unknown toward oneness with the One.

How can you navigate life on the basis of something as elusive as joy? It is quite simple.

The path to God is the path of joy. It may derive from being transported by a magnificent piece of music or a ladybug on a leaf. You may experience joy as a result of prayer or meditation. You may be joyful because you acted from unconditional love or nurtured the light within another. Joy may overwhelm you when you recognize in an instant the innumerable blessings that grace your life.

If days and weeks go by without your experiencing joy, you have taken a detour off the path to spirit. If the demands of the day fill your calendar, leaving no opportunity for you to renew yourself and refresh your spirit, start saying no to a few of them or find another way to get them done. Then use the time you have freed up to do something that gives you joy. If you have been taking steps on what you believe to be your spiritual path, but you are sad and tired and humorless because of it all, it is not your path to spirit.

God is all love and light, peace and joy. If you are experiencing more of that in your life, you are moving closer to spirit. If you experience it only rarely, you need to engage in some mid-course correction. If you do not experience it at all, you are walking the path of your immediate material reality. That gets you nowhere but leaves you exhausted and unfulfilled.

Joy is available to you every moment of every day. It surrounds you because God surrounds you. Choose to be joyful, as much and as often as you can. Then whatever steps you take will naturally lead you to spirit. Your joy will guide you there.

CHANGE

We have been describing the principles of evolution toward spirit. And evolution is all about change.

Or is it?

It all depends on what you believe changes and what you believe stays the same.

Change involves altering something from one state or form of being to another. In many ways all of life is changing all the time. Your body constantly creates new cells and sloughs off old ones. You develop new thoughts, experience new events, feel new emotions. To be alive is to change.

Or is it?

The spirit within you remains unchanged, with no regard to what you do or how you do it. No matter how much you move and adapt and renew, God's love and light shine inside you. The source of your life is God, and that source does not vary from one lifetime to the next or one individual to the next. God is a constant within all of life.

So, to be alive is to be God, and from that perspective

to be alive is not to change.

God has existed since before the beginning of creation and will exist beyond the end of creation. During that infinity of timelessness and spacelessness, God has remained and will remain unchanged.

God is. God is not becoming.

But you are becoming God.

You are being challenged to set aside the limitations imposed upon you by your third-dimensional reality. You are being asked to address the patterns you brought into this lifetime from earlier embodiments and heal them. You are expected to pay attention to everything you think and do. And when you find that it is lacking in or devoid of spirit, you must make modifications. All of that requires change.

Such change is necessary because your spirit has not yet evolved to oneness with God. The end point of your journey is union with the One in a perpetually unchanged state.

You must change in order, finally, not to.

BENEDICTION

For aeons we have been moving toward the light. Inch by inch we have offered our gifts and have seen intermittent progress. We have also seen regression. Nonetheless, those times did not concern us. For we know that extreme darkness is often a necessary precursor to a leap forward.

Planet earth is at another such point of rebirth. We see what you can and will accomplish. We are here to support you in your mission. We love you for the sacrifices you are making to be here at this moment in time.

We embrace the evolutionary path that you are pursuing. For as you know, it is impossible to stimulate global transformation without first—and all along the way—working on your own transformation. We recognize how dedicated you are to your own inner development. We also acknowledge your focus on the larger mission, which becomes more central with each passing day.

You have learned that change occurs slowly and with considerable resistance. You also know that what you envision is actually rooted in ancient wisdom. It is the manifestation of the larger reality beyond the veil. It is the force of interconnectedness that redefines relationships, whether they are person-to-person or person-to-nature. It is the One among the many.

Rejoice in the unprecedented quantity and quality of souls who are working with you in and out of embodiment to bring about the renewal of human experience on planet earth. Your work is progressing apace. You have colleagues and collaborators at every turn. You have our support in everything you do. We share the same vision and are committed to the same purpose.

Follow your heart. Listen to your truth. Acknowledge your capacities. Value your fellow pilgrims. Allow light and love to flow through you. Walk with joy in your steps and music in your heart.

We love you beyond eternity. We surround you with golden light. We share our joy and our blessings with you. We love. We love.

Gates McKibbin never imagined that after spending twenty years as a corporate executive, management consultant and adjunct college professor specializing in strategic and organizational renewal, she would publish messages channeled from her deceased father, John McKibbin. For most of her adult life she had balanced a fulfilling professional career and a fascinating spiritual quest. Then quite unexpectedly her father, who visited the earth plane frequently after his death, began sending telepathic messages for her to write in her journal.

Three years and six books later, Gates has now added "Inspirational author and speaker" to her resume. She still helps business executives navigate turbulent change, and she also seeds the planet with insights from the spirit world. To complement the LifeLines Library, Gates has developed a collection of thematic LifeLines note pads featuring her favorite one-liners from the books.

Born and raised in central Illinois, Gates now resides in San Francisco. Whenever she has a few hours of free time, she hunts for vintage jackets, walks to North Beach restaurants for risotto, creates bead-bedecked greeting cards and, of course, continues her journal writing. Gates holds a Ph.D. from the University of Illinois and has received numerous academic awards, among them Phi Beta Kappa.

LIFELINES LIBRARY ORDER FORM

FEATURING BOOKS BY GATES McKIBBIN

Book Title	Quantity	Total Cost
The Light in the Living Room: Dad's Messages from the Other Side $9.95		
LoveLines: Notes on Loving and Being Loved $9.95		
A Course in Courage: Disarming the Darkness with Strength of Heart $9.95		
A Handbook on Hope: Fusing Optimism and Action $9.95		
The Life of the Soul: The Path of Spirit in Your Lifetimes $9.95		
Available Wisdom: Insights from Beyond the Third Dimension $9.95		
Complete set of six books in the LifeLines Library $39.95		
Subtotal		
CA residents add 7.35% sales tax		
Postage and handling (F.O.B.)		
Total		

Payment Information

Charge to: VISA ☐ MasterCard ☐

Card number ______________________ Exp. date________

Ship to:

Name____

Street______________________________ Apt.________

City_________________________ State______ Zip________

Phone: ___________________ Fax___________________

E-mail: ______________________________________

To order by phone call (707) 433-9771

Fax your order to (707) 433-9772

Order via e-mail at www.fieldflowers.com

Visit our Website at www.lifelineslibrary.com

LIFELINES NOTE PADS ORDER FORM

FEATURING MESSAGES FROM BOOKS IN THE LIFELINES LIBRARY

Note Pads **12 messages in each pad, 108 pages**	**Quantity**	**Total Cost** **@ $7.95/pad**
Authenticity (#LL1000)		
Boundaries (#LL1001)		
Change (#LL1002)		
Commitment (#LL1003)		
Companionship (#LL1004)		
Courage (#LL1005)		
Effectiveness (#LL1006)		
Hope (#LL1007)		
Love (#LL1008)		
Real Work (#LL1009)		
Strength (#LL1010)		
Time (#LL1011)		
Unconditional Love (#LL1012)		
Vitality (#LL1013)		
Wisdom (#LL1014)		
Subtotal		
CA residents add 7.35% sales tax		
Postage and handling (F.O.B.)		
Total		

Payment Information

Charge to: VISA ☐ MasterCard ☐

Card number ______________________ Exp. date________

Ship to:

Name______________________________________

Street______________________________ Apt.________

City________________________ State______ Zip________

Phone: ____________________ Fax__________________

E-mail: ____________________________________

To order by phone call (707) 433-9771

Fax your order to (707) 433-9772

Order via e-mail at **www.fieldflowers.com**

Visit our Website at **www.lifelineslibrary.com**